香港國際詩歌之夜 2013
INTERNATIONAL POETRY NIGHTS IN HONG KONG

編輯 Editors

北島 Bei Dao

陳嘉恩 Shelby K. Y. Chan

方梓勳 Gilbert C. F. Fong

柯夏智 Lucas Klein

馬德松 Christopher Mattison

康慈天娜・告魯茲
Conchitina Cruz

目錄 Contents

1 Exhibition Notes

At six I lost my first watch and gave up on biking. At eight I wanted a cow and a fridge to put the cow's food in, and also a music box. At thirteen I broke a tooth in a dream and for days tapped each tooth in my mouth with my tongue, searching for cracks. At seventeen I lived with three strangers and at twenty-one I got chicken pox exactly two weeks before graduation. I prefer beer to wine. I prefer a couch to a chaise longue. I prefer landmarks to street signs. I prefer to say perhaps rather than maybe, which perhaps makes me sound officious, although I hope this is not the case. I like to watch horse races and figure skaters. I like not being good friends with my neighbors. When in the shower, I sing. When afflicted with a pain I have no name for, I sleep it off. I cry over migraines and missed deadlines. I would rather rent for life than be responsible for a house. I would rather spend a weekend up in the mountains than in the city, but this was not always so. I look forward to plane rides, if they are less than ten hours long. On trips I prefer to stay in the hotel and read books, often about the place I am visiting. I like to sit in the lobby and take pictures of window views. I do not mind asking strangers for directions. I do not get upset when the directions turn out to be unreliable. I do not think twice about spending money on books, but I tend to hold off on buying a bag of potato chips, no matter how intriguing the flavor. Sometimes, in my office, I choose not to answer the knock at the door, despite its persistence. I pretend I am asleep, or simply not there. I find turnstiles and carousels reassuring. I think photographs of shadows are inevitably elegant. There were years when I signed my name as well as the date and place of purchase in every book I bought, and there were years I did not. There were years I recorded in my journals and there were years I did not. I enjoy sitting in a coffee shop and listening to the talk at the next table, but I am annoyed when I tell my companion a joke and find the man at the next table laughing. I cannot look at a painting without reading its title first. I feel awkward making the sign of the cross. I feel compelled to write words with my index finger on dusty surfaces. I do not smoke pot if there is no one in the room I would like to sleep with. Mannequins make me nervous, as do poorly ventilated diners. I am always a little disappointed when the person I am calling picks up the phone. I have a hard time watching movies with scenes of rape and torture in them. I would rather not have a conversation begin with "We need to talk," although experience has taught me that what follows is not necessarily terrible news. There are two or three things in my life that I regret. I am pro-choice but am amenable to a reproductive health law that excludes abortion. I am embarrassed to belong to one of two countries in the world with no divorce law. I read the news after I read the classifieds. I despise cops and evangelists. I can live without beauty pageants, although I find myself keeping the television on long enough to see the evening gown portion. Sometimes, alone in a restaurant, I feel obliged to finish my food quickly if there are others waiting to be seated. I stay away from people who hand out flyers. I stop in front of pet shops when rabbits and birds are on display. I compare prices. I make lists. I return by the due date. I think it is better to walk in the middle of the street and get hit by a car than to walk on a dark sidewalk and get mugged. I think a cab with a rosary hanging from its rearview mirror is safer to ride in than a cab without it. I have a hard time evading small talk. I have fallen down a flight of stairs twice. I have watched a group of men smash a car with lead pipes. I have stood on top of a mountain in one country to view the mountains of another. I have had sex in ten countries across four continents. I have been kissed inappropriately by a priest. When I am bewildered I think of olive trees half my size which I must have seen on a trip long ago or merely read about. When I am unnerved I recite the phone numbers I know by heart and am relieved that I still know them. There are two or three things I have done that I must apologize for. I sleep by myself on the right side of a double bed. I sleep with the lights off, and by this I mean I sleep with the light from the lamppost outside my window. When a man is in bed with me I leave the cat outside and ignore its meowing by the door. When a man is in bed with me I say screw even when make love is a distinct possibility. There were years I spent filled with road rage and there were years I did not. There were years I wrote thank you notes and snacked on cheese and crackers and there were years I did not. I do not underestimate receptionists and security guards. I am more likely to pick up a book with a beautiful cover even if it is by an unknown author than a book with a hideous cover even if it is by an author I love. I think dictionaries are more reliable than novels. I think swimming pools are far more bearable than oceans. I forgive friends easily, but I am a ruthless critic of acquaintances. I am sometimes rendered speechless by indecision. Sometimes, on my way to work, I see myself walking across the street. I feel the urge to follow myself, but soon enough, I change my mind.

展品説明

六歲我弄丟了我的手錶，放棄了騎自行車。八歲我想要一頭母牛和一台用來放母牛食物的冰箱，以及一個八音盒。十三歲我在夢中弄碎一顆牙，之後的幾天，我都用舌頭輕扣每一顆牙，尋找裂紋。十七歲我和三個陌生人同住。二十一歲我畢業前剛好兩個星期得了水痘。我喜歡啤酒勝於葡萄酒。喜歡沙發勝於臥榻。喜歡地標勝於街上的標識。我喜歡説「可能」勝過説「或許」，「可能」聽上去很隨意，儘管我希望並非如此。我喜歡看賽馬和花樣滑冰。我不喜歡和鄰居做好朋友。洗澡時我唱歌。如果我遭受無名的痛，我會把它睡過去。我哭到偏頭痛，錯過了截止日期。我寧願租房住，而不是買個房子來負責。我寧願在山裏而不是城裏度週末，但也不總這樣。如果機程短於十小時，我期待飛機旅行。旅途中，我喜歡呆在酒店讀書，關於此處我正造訪的地方的書。我喜歡坐在大堂拍攝窗外的景色。我不介意向陌生人問路。當問來的路越走越不對時，我也不會沮喪。買書時我不假思索地付錢，但買一包薯片，無論那口味多誘人，我都會猶豫不決。有時，在辦公室裏，我會不回應敲門聲，無論那人敲多久。我假裝睡著了或壓根不在屋裏。我發現十字轉門和旋轉木馬令人安心。我認為拍影子的照片無可避免地優雅。有好幾年，我在新買的書上簽下自己的名字和購買時的時間地點，好幾年我又不這麼做。有好幾年，我用日記做記錄，好幾年又不這麼做。我喜歡坐在咖啡店聽鄰桌說話。但當我和朋友說笑話時，要是鄰桌笑了，我就會惱怒。不讀一幅畫的標題，我就沒法看這幅畫。劃十字時我感覺尷尬。用食指在沾滿灰塵的表面寫字時，我會有種強迫感。如果房間裏沒有我想和他一起睡的人，我就不抽大麻。人體模特讓我緊張，通風不良的小餐館也是。我給他打電話的那個人接聽時，我總是感到一點失望。看有強姦和酷刑畫面的電影會令我感到十分難捱。我寧願不要進行那些第一句是「我們需要談談」的談話，雖然經驗告訴我接下來聽到的消息未必糟糕。生命中有兩三件事令我後悔。我擁護自由選擇墮胎，但卻覺得自己適合一部不含墮胎的生殖健康法。我尷尬於自己生活在世界上兩個不允許離婚的國家之一。我讀完分類廣告再讀新聞。我鄙視警察和傳福音者。我的生活中可以沒有選美，即使我發現自己一直開著電視看關於晚裝的節目。有時，一人在餐館吃飯，如果有人等位子，我就覺得自己有義務趕快吃完。我繞開派發廣告傳單的人。我駐足在寵物店的櫥窗前，要是那裏有兔子和鳥。我比較價格。我列清單。我在最後期限前歸還物品。我認為走在馬路中間被車撞倒好過走在陰暗的人行道上被搶劫。我覺得那些後視鏡上掛著玫瑰吊飾的出租車比沒有吊飾的更安全。我一度艱難地避免隨便聊聊。我從飛機階梯上摔下來過兩次。我目睹過一群男人用鉛管砸一輛車。我曾站在山頂上從一個國家去望另一個國家的山。我在四個大洲十個國家做過愛。我被一位牧師不恰當地吻過。當我不知所措，就會想到高度是我一半的那些橄欖樹，我一定在很久以前的一次旅行中見過它們，或者只是讀到過它們。當我焦慮時，我會默誦心裏記住的電話號碼，並因我仍然記得它們而感到安慰。有兩、三件事我必須為我做過它們而道歉。我獨自睡在雙人床的右邊。我熄燈睡覺，這樣也就意味著窗外的燈火陪伴著我的睡眠。當一個男人與我同睡，我會把貓留在門外，忽略它在門邊喵喵聲。當一個男人與我同睡，即使明顯可能可以稱為做愛我也會說幹。好些年我駕車時憤懣滿胸，好些年又不這樣。好些年我寫感謝字條，吃芝士和餅乾當零食，好些年又不這樣。我不低估前台人員和保安。我更傾向於選一本封面漂亮的書，即使它出自一位不知名的作者，也不會選一本我愛的作家寫的但封面很醜的書。我認為字典比小說更值得信賴。我認為游泳池比海洋更容易忍受。我輕易原諒朋友，但對熟人是個無情的批評家。我有時優柔寡斷講不出什麼意見。有時在上班路上，我看見自己在過馬路。我感到一種衝動要去跟上自己，但很快，我就會打消了這個念頭。

（曹疏影、朱曉玢譯）

2 Letter to the Stranger

1

What I am about to tell you may or may not matter in the long run.

2

I have taken to alphabetizing the things in my kitchen. Thus colander next to coriander, dairy next to dishwashing liquid, ice next to insecticide. Anything can be held together by a web of associations: armoire to banister, by virtue of setting. Clavicle to daffodil, by family of sounds. Elephants to falafel because of that day in December, gash to harbor because of that summer with nothing better to do. Illicit to jeopardy, jeopardy to karma, karma to long life or lip service or manual labor, manual labor to never again, never again to on one condition to private practice to questionnaire. And so on. Anything is the truest beginning of what I am about to say.

3

Words most probably included in what I am about to tell you: accept, again, alcohol, apparently, bakery, be, because, blue, bordering, come, company, continuous, crap, dashboard, definitely, don't, drawer, end, enough, exactly, fantasy, forget, haha, how, hydrangeas, ink, insult, maybe, modern, more, must, nerve, never, no, of, period, phone, please, psycho, ridiculous, ring, slab, sleeping, sorry, splat, stash, teeth, television, tender, then, there, this, though, thus, very, wtf, yes.

4

What I am about to say may be said in other words, and these words may be divided into several categories resembling a system of looking at flies: a) detached, with a hint of disdain, b) obligatory, c) doubt replaced by candor, d) having slipped from one room to another, e) borrowed from the library, f) a subcategory of c), g) that which replays itself, h) without resignation.

給陌生人的信

一

我所要告訴你的，也許事關長遠，也許不是。

二

我在廚房裏按字母順序擺放物品。這樣，笊籬旁是香菜，乳品旁邊是洗潔精，冰塊旁邊是殺蟲劑。任何東西都可用某種關聯組織起來：大衣櫥到樓梯欄杆，是通過美德的設定；鎖骨到水仙，是通過家中的聲音。從大象到蔬菜炸丸子，是因為十二月的一天，從傷口到港口，是因為沒什麼其他事可做的夏天。從非法不當到危險，從危險到因果，從因果到漫長人生或應酬話或體力勞動，從體力勞動到絕不再來，從絕不再來到某個條件下到私人執業到問卷。等等如此類推。每件事物都是我要談到的事物的最真實的開端。

三

我要告訴你的事物中，最可能包括的詞彙有：接受、再次、酒精、顯然地、麵包店、是、因為、藍、邊緣、來、陪伴、持續的、廢話、儀錶板、毫無疑問、不要、抽屜、結束、足夠、確實地、幻想、忘記、哈哈、怎樣、水仙花屬、墨水、侮辱、也許、現代、更多、必須、神經、絕不、不、的、時期、電話、請、精神病、荒謬的、戒指、平板、睡覺、對不起、圖示、隱藏、牙齒、電視、溫和的、然後、那裏、這個、雖然、如此、非常、見鬼、是的。

四

我要告訴你的，也許可以用其他詞彙來説，這些詞彙也許分成若干類別，和觀看廣告單張的系統相似：a) 分離，用輕蔑的暗示，b) 義不容辭，c) 用坦率取代的懷疑，d) 從一間房間滑到另一間房間，e) 從圖書館借書，f) 一個次分類，g) 重播本身，h) 辭職。

（曹疏影、朱曉玢譯）

3 Here

In Manila, I spend an inordinate amount of time
around copy machines.
In the cheap hotel, I peel an apple with a Swiss knife.
In my childhood bedroom, I weep over an
unpresentable pincushion made for sewing class.
In Bali, I am too embarrassed to say no to a manicure.
In Makati, I take off my heels and slip into flats.
In the coffee shop, I write the incriminating postcard.
In the ballet studio, I am amused by my catastrophic
pirouettes.
In Chicago, I attempt to mimic an old roommate's
unidentifiable accent.
In Bangkok, I am addressed in Chinese.
In the computer room, I read the signs.
In the government office, I apologize for the errors on
the form.
In Bellagio, I am mistaken for the writing resident's
companion.
In the arctic conference room, I am intrigued by the
red telephone.
In Los Angeles, I am thought to be Mexican.

In the elevator, I smile at the child drooling in its
stroller.
In Rome, I am unfazed by the transport strike.
In Palawan, I take my lunch with a bottle of cerveza.
In the rickety cable car, I admit to my unforgivable
condescension.
In Singapore, I think of Cubao in June.
In Venice, I watch a poodle sashay toward an ice cream
shop.
In the library, I hunt in sequence, from PN to PQ to
PR.
In my office, I am annoyed by the display of privilege
in texts about travel.
In Boracay, I try to appreciate the Victorian wallpaper.
In the taxi, I am asked an unnerving question.
In Mandaluyong, I admire a strongly worded memo.
In Sendai, I distract myself by painting flowers on a
handkerchief.
In Brisbane, I am thrilled to spot an actor whose
movies I abhor.
In the theater, I am envious of the protagonist's

impeccable posture.
In New York City, I procrastinate.
In church, I calculate the costs of moving to a bigger
apartment.
In the balcony, I doze during a mellow card game.
In Dumaguete, I affectionately decline phone sex at
two in the morning.
In the clinic, I am pressured by the clerk to hyphenate.
In Florence, I lose a coat.
In the allegedly ghost-ridden hallway, I am hungry
after making out.
In Binondo, I reject my companion's dining choices.
In Paris, I purchase tokens for a five-minute shower.
In Amsterdam, I am seized by an uncharacteristic
confusion over left and right.
In Cleveland, I excuse myself from the exasperating
religious debate over dinner.
In Tokyo, I am asked to produce too many
identification cards to have my money changed.
In the hole in the wall, I wear my interlocutor's
sunglasses.

In Cubao, I call into question the sparseness of my
wardrobe.
In the supermarket, I comfort myself in the aisle
devoted to cleaning agents.
In Baguio, I eat a macaroon.
In Antipolo, I learn to make a rosary, a macramé belt,
and a hand-sewn apron.
In Pittsburgh, I adopt a cat.
In the waiting room, I judge the painting on the wall.
In the bungalow by the beach, I indulge in the delusion
of a miniature herb garden.
In Davao, I despair over the malfunctioning keycard.
In Los Baños, I am told to keep my voice down.

這裏

在馬尼拉，我在複印機前花費出奇多的時間。
在廉價旅店，我用瑞士軍刀削蘋果皮。
在童年的臥室，我為一個為縫紉課準備的不成樣子
　　的針線團而哭。
在峇厘島，我尷尬得不能對一位修甲師說不。
在馬卡蒂，我脫下高跟鞋，溜進房間。
在咖啡店，我寫認罪的明信片。
在芭蕾房，我被我災難性的轉腳尖逗樂了。
在芝加哥，我試著模仿一位老室友難以辨認的口
　　音。
在曼谷，我穿成中國人的樣子。
在電腦室，我閱讀符號。
在政府辦公室，我為表格上的錯誤道歉。
在百樂宮酒店，我被誤認為是那位作家客人的同
　　伴。
在北極會議室，我被那部紅色電話引發好奇心。
在洛杉磯，我被認做墨西哥人。
在電梯裏，我對著嬰兒車裏流口水的孩子微笑。
在羅馬，我未受交通罷工的影響。
在巴拉望島，我邊吃午餐邊喝一瓶啤酒。

在搖搖晃晃的纜車裏，我承認自己帶有不可寬恕的高姿態。

在新加坡，我想起六月的奎松。

在威尼斯，我看一條貴婦狗走向雪糕店。

在圖書館，我按順序找書，從PN到PQ到PR。

在辦公室，我被旅行文章裏表現出來的特權惹惱了。

在長灘島，我試著欣賞維多利亞風格的壁紙。

在出租車裏，我被問到一個令人不安的問題。

在曼達盧永，我喜歡一張言辭強烈的便條。

在仙台，我被手帕上畫著的花朵分散了注意力。

在布里斯本，我竟然認出一個演員，他的電影我很討厭。

在劇院裏，我羨慕主角那完美無瑕的姿態。

在紐約，我拖延。

在教堂裏，我計算著搬去一間更大的公寓要花的費用。

在陽臺上，我在玩熟了的紙牌遊戲時打瞌睡。

在杜馬格特，我在凌晨兩點親切地拒絕了電話性愛。

在診所，我因職員的斷字感到壓力。
在佛羅倫斯，我丟了一件大衣。
在據說有鬼出沒的門廳，我弄清情況後感到一陣肚餓。
在唐人街，我否定了同伴選擇的食物。
在巴黎，我為洗五分鐘淋浴而購買代幣。
在阿姆斯特丹，我陷入了不知關於左右的無名困惑之中。
在克利夫蘭，我避開晚餐時那次可氣的宗教辯論。
在東京，我去換錢時被要求出示過多的身份證明。
在牆上的洞裏，我戴上交談者的墨鏡。
在奎松，我開始對自己不那麼滿的衣櫃生疑。
在超級市場，我在放清潔劑的過道上安撫自己。
在碧瑤，我吃了一塊馬卡龍點心。
在安迪波洛，我學做一朵玫瑰，一條花邊帶子，和手縫一條圍裙。
在匹茲堡，我領養了一隻貓。
在等候室，我品評牆上的畫。
在沙灘上的小房子裏，我縱情於迷你植物園帶來的幻覺中。

在達沃，我對失靈的門卡感到失望。
在洛斯巴諾斯，我被要求降低音量。

（曹疏影、朱曉玢譯）

4 Half an Hour in the House of Indecision or Procrastination

ants

The cotton buds are attracting ants by the hundreds, they are almost flowers.

blinds

The blinds are behaving like piano keys at the mercy of an inebriated player. Or: the blinds are undulating like the sea on an uneventful summer day. Or: the blinds are shimmering like grass skirt of a woman scavenging for keys in a cavernous purse.

conundrum

Are there three illegal puppies yelping without let up in the apartment next door or just two?

electric fan

The dust clinging to the spokes of the fan spans several eras: The Era of the Apartment Devastated by Flood, The Era of Politically Incorrect Yet Extremely Amusing Terms for Informal Settlers, and The Era of Citrus-

Scented Cleaning Agents to Cover Up the Accidents of the Ailing Cat.

insight
Instant coffee with condensed milk is too pleasant to be thought of as making do.

history
There is nothing in the house that seems to have emerged from a grandmotherly chest inlaid with mother-of-pearl save for the stereoscope and the box of slides of pastoral scenes in turn-of-the-century India.

melodica
In lieu of the guitar left in the office. In lieu of the sorely missed cable subscription. In lieu of mid-week nights at the bar with unexplainably cheap margaritas, now closed for renovation.

note
The term you mean to use when you say *threshed out* is *fleshed out.*

shameful vanity
The photograph taken years ago to commemorate the literary tattoo is languishing in a book bag from a forgettable conference.

wishful thinking
Today is hopefully not the day the landlady slips the electric bill under the door.

優柔寡斷者或拖延症患者的房中半小時

螞蟻

棉籤引來幾百隻螞蟻，他們幾乎是花朵了。

百葉窗

百葉窗在動作，如同微醺者心懷溫柔彈起的琴鍵。或：百葉窗在起伏，如同平靜夏日裏的海。或：百葉窗微光閃閃，如同正在手袋裏翻鑰匙的女人的草裙。

難題

隔壁寓所一直大吠著的小狗是三隻還是兩隻？

電扇

風扇葉片上的塵埃正跨越幾個時代：公寓毀於洪水的時代，非正規居民條款政治不正確、卻極有趣味的時代，用柑橘味清潔劑掩蓋病貓事故的時代。

洞察

速溶咖啡加煉乳，實在太美妙了，沒人想到這是人造的。

歷史

屋子裏，沒有什麼好像是從鑲著珍珠母的祖母般的胸前顯露出來的，那為一隻立體鏡和一盒世紀之交的印度田園風光幻燈片所保存著的東西。

口風琴

替代那把留在辦公室的吉他。

替代那不該錯過的有線電視。

替代一個星期中間幾天在那家酒吧度過的夜晚，那裏有出奇便宜的瑪格麗特酒，而現在它關門裝修了。

筆記

當你說「推敲」時，你的意思是「充實」。

可恥的虛榮

幾年前拍下的那幅照片，為的是紀念紋在身上的文字。而今，它在一隻書包裏褪色，已經不記得那是哪次會議上得到的書包了。

願望

希望今天不會是房東太太把電費單塞在門底下的那天。

（曹疏影、朱曉玢譯）

5 Five Lines

I'm spying on myself again.
I'm slicing tomatoes and tossing the chunks in a bowl.
The kitchen light is attentive, and so is the blue of the bowl.
Now must be the safest time to disappear.
I won't come out until I'm gone.

五行詩

我再次監視我自己。
我把番茄切片，又搖搖碗裏的番茄塊。
廚房的燈光溫柔，碗的藍色也是。
現在一定是用來消失最安全的時間。
而直到我徹底消失我才會出來。

（曹疏影、朱曉玢譯）

6 Signals

I took the amaretto to mean there was no beer in the
house.
I took the bassline to mean a particular addressee was
in the crowd.
I took the clairvoyant weather to mean I could dismiss
your unappealing conclusions.
I took the dry run to mean the echo was unreliable.
I took the elevated appeal of allusions to mean the fever
had no fangs.
I took your fury to mean there was grass in the
basement.
I took the gelatinous substance to mean a diminished
generosity toward herbivorous endeavors.
I took happiness to mean I had the right syllable in
mind.
I took the initials to mean just leave the front door
unlocked.
I took the jellyfish scuttling by the reef to mean the
kleptomania was the least of my concerns.
I took the kiss to mean a potentially inconsequential
lesson.

I took the lesion barely hidden by your sleeve to mean
you had no wish to mimic the tragedies of your
flawed heroines.
I took the marionette on the clothesline to mean there
was hope for the unsuspecting neighbor.
I took no to mean it was the only answer.
I took the oppressive serendipity to mean that
panic might or might not send us straight into an
emergency.
I took the paprika to mean quiz the cook, not the
gardener.
I took the imperious quill to mean the repetition was
intentional.
I took the sly reference to mean the substitute had
surpassed the preference.
I took the song to mean you took the necessary pill.
I took the tricky decimal to mean I should unsay the
speech I made over dinner.
I took the unexpected unification to mean veer away
from condescending middlemen.
I took the violinist's lisp to mean it was imperative to

wait in line.
I took the waiver to mean there was a xenophobe in the
building.
I took the third x-ray to mean you had nothing more
to lose.
I took the yapping from the room below to mean the
token zorroing was a far more appropriate gesture.
I took the zero dangling from the headline to mean the
aphorism was a spell in disguise.

信號

我用苦杏仁酒來表明屋裏沒有啤酒。
我彈起貝斯音線來表明人群中有個特別的收件人。
我享受清澈透明的好天氣來表明我可以解構你乏味
的結論。
我用排練來表明迴響是靠不住的。
我放大典故的魅力來表明狂熱沒有獠牙。
我承受你的憤怒來表明地下室有草生長。
我接受膠狀物來表明越來越不寬容食素的努力。
我用快樂來表明我心中懷有正確的音節。
我只寫縮寫來表明我剛剛並未鎖上前門。
我撿起被礁石刺穿的水母來表明我並不關心盜竊
癖。
我接吻來表明一個實際上無關緊要的教訓。
我露出就藏在你袖子裏的傷痕來表明你並不想去模
仿你那問題女主角的悲劇。
我拿起繫在晾衣繩上的木偶來表明期待可以信賴的
鄰居。
我說不，來表明這就是唯一的答案。
我接受沉重的意外發現來表明恐慌可能或不可能直
接把我們帶入緊急狀況。
我拿來辣椒表明要測驗的是廚師，而非園丁。

我拿起傲慢的鵝毛筆來表明重複是故意的。
我舉出狡猾的參照物來表明替代品蓋過偏好。
我唱起這首歌表明你吃了必須要吃的藥片。
我打下詭計多端的小數點來表明我應該撤回自己在晚餐上說的那一番話。
我用出人意料的聯合來表明從傲慢的中間人那裏逃脱。
我像小提琴手那樣口齒不清，是表明必須排隊等候。
我用棄權來表明大廈裏瀰漫著一種仇外。
我接受第三次X光檢查表明你再沒什麼可以失去了。
我接受樓下房間的哇哇聲表明Z形運動是更為合適的姿勢。
我讓標題裏的0搖擺晃蕩表明那句格言不過是托詞。

（曹疏影、朱曉玢譯）

7 A Field Guide to Neighborhood Flora and Fauna on the Last Day of 2009

atis

The lampposts are infested with staple wires and sprouting want ads for plumbers. They are upstaging the curvy globes of atis hanging from trees.

bougainvilleas

What a house with a blue roof, blue shutters, and a blue door needs are bougainvilleas in a row of blue pots.

commerce

They suggested cabbage, cell phone plans, or a cheap ride home. She asked for forget-me-nots, but they unfortunately did not speak flower.

dead tree

The cops are finally noticing the dead tree, its brittle branches trapped in a cat's cradle of cable wires. Or maybe they are merely admiring the blimp afloat in a sea of cumulus clouds.

devotion

The store they run is always out of eggs, noodles, and sardines. They're always tossing their trash in the canal by their fence. She's always yelling on the phone and he's always harping about the hens across the street. But every morning the old couple take their five shih tzus out into the sunlight, sit them one by one on a stool, and comb their long blond hair.

fried fish

It's one thing to turn a corner and find a feral face painted on the hood of an orange car. It's another to take money out of a machine and detect the smell of fried fish.

kalamansi

The overpopulated kalamansi plant is now serving you with delight!

loan sharks

Of course, it would be best to avoid them.

Penelope the piglet

Penelope the piglet is hanging by the ears from the clothesline and hooting at the neighborhood kids.

She says, "That is one fashionable strawberry blond wig!"
She says, "It was Hawksmoor, with his non-intrusive freemasonry references in structures, who taught me the possibilities of art in architecture."
She says, "Look at the silly dogs on the ledge!"
She says, "I want to sodomize you in your sleep."

road kill

Today's view from the congee place is of two kids in the middle of the road, poking at unidentifiable road kill. Is it too much to ask for this not to be so?

strays

Every so often, on the news, they feature stray cats being sold by the sackful.

whiskers

Aside from decks, yellow bell canopies are most fashionable in the neighborhood. And also the bushes of nameless white flowers, the ones with whiskers so friendly and flailing in the sun.

yin and yang

A scruffy black dog in white socks is sleeping under a car. A scrawny white dog in a black mask is telepathing dreams of dinner.

2009年最後一天，鄰居植物小姐和動物先生的野外指南

番荔枝

燈柱纏滿馬蹄釘，萌生一則則水管工徵聘廣告。它們在同懸於枝頭的番荔枝那圓潤的球形搶鏡頭。

簕杜鵑

藍屋頂、藍窗、藍色大門，這樣的一座房子，需要一排藍花盆裏的簕杜鵑。

商務

他們推薦大白菜，手機套餐計劃，以及可省錢的騎車回家。她想要勿忘我，但很不幸，他們並未提到鮮花。

死樹

警察終於注意到這株死樹。它易碎的枝條困在一隻電線編製的貓咪搖籃裏。又或者，他們只是喜歡欣賞雲海裏浮遊的飛艇。

忠誠

他們的店鋪裏，雞蛋、麵條和沙丁魚總是缺貨。他們總是從柵欄內向運河裏扔垃圾。她總是對電話大嚷大叫，而他總是過馬路時對母雞喋喋不休。然而，每天早上，這對老夫妻牽出他們的五條西施犬，走進晨光，讓牠們一條條在凳子上坐好，為牠們梳理那長而金色的毛髮。

煎魚

拐個彎，找到畫在那輛橙色汽車車蓋上的野性蓬勃的臉，這是一回事。從機器裏取出錢，並發覺煎魚的氣味，這是另一回事。

金桔

這棵果實累累的金桔樹，正興高采烈地為您服務！

高利貸者

當然，避開他們是最好的。

小豬佩妮洛普

耳朵掛在晾衣繩上，小豬佩妮洛普正呵斥鄰居的孩子們。

她說：「這是一頂時髦的草莓金色的假髮！」

她說：「是霍克斯穆爾和他在結構中的非侵入性共濟會參照，教給我建築中藝術的可能性。」

她說：「看窗台上那些傻狗！」

她說：「我想在你睡覺時雞姦你。」

街殺

今天，從粥鋪裏望出去的景象是馬路中間的兩個孩子，指著街上被車軋死的難以辨認的動物屍體。若叫這件事不要這樣，是否過分？

流浪貓

隔不了多久，新聞裏，就會出現一整袋在出售的流浪貓。

鬚

甲板旁邊，黃鐘罩是這附近最時尚的東西。還有不知名的白色花叢，它們友好的細鬚在陽光中輕舞。

陰陽

一隻穿白襪子的邋遢黑狗在汽車底睡著。一隻骨瘦如豺的白狗正在牠的黑面具下，做著關於晚餐的美夢。

（曹疏影、朱曉玢譯）

8 Two or Three Things about Desire

Sunlight half-preening, almost fashionable.
An hour removed from this angle and cocotte becomes
you.
I fish a kiss out of your river: o miss demeanor, o
misdemeanor.
Nothing like leafy limbs clattering in attendance.
Really now, I say, perpendicular to your purplish
dream.

慾望二三事

日光半妝，幾乎時尚。
自此角度，移走一小時，妓女變成你。
我從你的河流中釣起一個吻，哦小姐風采，哦一次
　　小罪。
沒有什麼像那多葉的枝幹，出場時嘩啦作響。
現在，真的，我說，垂直於你紫紅色的夢。

（曹疏影、朱曉玢譯）

9 Still Life with Playing Cards

At last, I am at my wit's end.
I deliver myself to the notary public on the sketchy side
of the neighborhood and at the entrance
I stand, anticipating my arrival.
There is an appropriate letter for every mishap.
I ask myself to choose a club: to enter,
to swing, to beat unabashedly.
As usual I am wary of my ideas.
Perhaps the club is a spade is a heart is a diamond
in disguise. As usual I agree with myself.
Money changes hands.

撲克靜物畫

最後，我智窮力竭。
趁旁邊的人不注意，我把自己
交給公證人，並且站在入口
期待自己的抵達。
每起災難都有一個相對應的字母。
我讓自己選擇一個梅花（俱樂部）：走進去，
搖擺，放開了打鼓。
像往常一樣，我提防著自己的想法。
也許這梅花就是黑桃就是紅心
就是偽裝的方塊。像往常一樣，我同意了我自己。
金錢轉手。

（曹疏影、朱曉玢譯）

10 Postcards from Here and There

Salutation. Alternate caption for image. Doodle + overexplanation. Rundown of schedule, token promise, hyperbolic expression of love. Yours,

* * *

Salutation. Description of cloud cover, choice beverage, current cast of strangers. Reference to season, clunky display of newly acquired vocabulary. Unreasonable query, half-hearted joke. Yours,

* * *

Salutation. Location and historical fact overheard at the station. Gratitude for phone call. Reiteration of gratitude. Comment on noise, comparison to random locations. Rejection of comments made thus far. Annoyance. Apology. Yours,

* * *

Salutation. Happiness over recent purchase. Slight nostalgia and paranoia. Recollection of code invented in grade school. Name in code. Name in code. Yours,

* * *

Salutation. Quote lifted from exhibit notes. Emphasis on *repeatable, reportable, impoverished, impartial.*

Deletion of *im*, note on nested words, *imp*, *impart*.

Yours,

Note:

Some of these poems have appeared, at times as slightly different versions, in the following journals:

Diagram: "Letter to the Stranger," "Postcards from Here and There"

Cordite Poetry Review: "Exhibition Notes," "Signals," "Half an Hour in the House of Indecision or Procrastination"

Salt Hill: "Five Lines"

The poem "Here" is forthcoming in *The Offending Adam*.

來自八方的明信片

稱謂。圖像的備用說明。塗鴉 + 過度詮釋。行程表，履行的承諾，愛的雙曲線表達。落款，

* * *

稱謂。雲層的描述，飲料選擇，陌生人的當下角色。季節參考，新識詞彙的笨拙展示。奇怪的詢問，三心二意的玩笑。落款，

* * *

稱謂。地點和在車站偷聽到的史實。感謝電話。重申感謝。噪音評論，隨機位置的比較。拒絕迄今為止的評論。煩人。道歉。落款，

* * *

稱謂。最近買到的幸福。些微懷鄉和偏執。重新收集小學時代發明的代碼。姓名代碼。姓名代碼。
落款，

* * *

稱謂。從展品說明裏摘出的字句。強調**可重複的(repeatable)**，**可報告的(reportable)**，**窮困的(impoverished)**，**公正無私的(impartial)**。刪除其前綴(im)，注意裏面嵌著的字，小惡魔(imp)，給予(impart)。落款，

（曹疏影、朱曉玢譯）

康慈天娜・告魯茲出生於菲律賓馬尼拉，在菲律賓大學迪利曼分校教授創意寫作和文學。她的詩歌作品包括獲得國家詩歌圖書獎的《黑暗時刻》(2005)、《別處徘徊》(2008)。告魯茲與阿當・大衛、德拉娜・阿奎拉合作出版了《克莉絲汀・阿貝拉壁櫥裏的服裝目錄——永久學生、烏凱粉絲和強迫性遊客》(2012)。她曾擔任*High Chair 12*的聯合編輯，該雜誌三分一內容為關注 2009 年馬京達瑙省大屠殺。告魯茲也是《Kritika Kultura 新菲律賓英文寫作選》（馬尼拉雅典耀大學英語系，2011 年3 月）的編輯之一。她是傅爾布萊特和洛克菲勒基金會的受資助人，她在菲律賓和美國期刊上發表詩作。她還和幾位馬尼拉詩人一起經營一家名為「青春美麗旅」(The Youth & Beauty Brigade) 的小型出版社。現在她正攻讀紐約州立大學奧爾巴尼分校的英語博士學位。

Conchitina Cruz was born in Manila. She teaches creative writing and literature at the University of the Philippines in Diliman. Her books of poetry include *Dark Hours* (UP Press, 2005), which received the National Book Award for Poetry, and *elsewhere held and lingered* (High Chair, 2008). Together with Adam David and Delilah Aguilar, she co-authored *A Catalogue of Clothes for Sale from the Closet of Christine Abella—Perpetual Student, Ukay Fan, and Compulsive Traveler* (The Youth & Beauty Brigade, 2012). She served as co-editor of *High Chair 12*, a three-part issue of the journal devoted to the Maguindanao Massacre of 2009, and the *Kritika Kultura Anthology of New Philippine Writing in English* (English Department, Ateneo de Manila University, March 2011). A recipient of Fulbright and Rockefeller Foundation grants, she has published her poetry in Philippine and American journals. Together with a few other Manila-based writers, Cruz runs a small press called The Youth & Beauty Brigade. She is currently pursuing a PhD in English at the University at Albany, The State University of New York.

出版 Publisher
香港中文大學出版社 The Chinese University Press

封面影像 Cover Image
北島 Bei Dao

出版日期 Date of Publication
二零一三年十一月 November 2013

國際書號 ISBN
978-962-996-613-3

香港國際詩歌之夜 2013 International Poetry Nights in Hong Kong 2013
主辦單位 Organizers
香港中文大學文學院 Faculty of Arts, The Chinese University of Hong Kong
香港浸會大學文學院 Faculty of Arts, Hong Kong Baptist University
香港科技大學人文社會科學學院 School of Humanities and Social Science, The Hong Kong University of Science and Technology

合作夥伴 In Partnership With
英國文化協會 British Council

協辦單位 Co-organizers
時刻文化 Moment Communications
香港中文大學出版社 The Chinese University Press

贊助 Sponsors
香港兆基創意書院 HKICC Lee Shau Kee School of Creativity
中國會 The China Club
周凱旋基金會 Chau Hoi Shuen Foundation

Printed in Hong Kong